ENERGIZE YOUR FINGERS EVERY DAY®

Helen Marlais

DAY ONE 1   DAY TWO 2   DAY THREE 3   DAY FOUR 4   DAY FIVE 5
★ LESSON DAY

THE
F·J·H
MUSIC
COMPANY
INC.
Frank J. Hackinson

Production: Frank J. Hackinson
Production Coordinators: Joyce Loke and Satish Bhakta
Cover: Terpstra Design, San Francisco
Cover and Interior Illustrations: Nina Victor Crittenden, Minneapolis, Minnesota
Text Design and Layout: Terpstra Design, Maritza Cosano Gomez, and Andi Whitmer
Engraving: Tempo Music Press, Inc.
Printer: Tempo Music Press, Inc.

ISBN-13: 978-1-61928-007-6

ABOUT THE AUTHOR

Dr. Marlais is one of the most prolific authors in the field of educational piano books and an exclusive writer for The FJH Music Company Inc. The critically acclaimed and award-winning piano series, *Succeeding at the Piano*® *A Method for Everyone*, *Succeeding with the Masters*®, *The Festival Collection*®, *In Recital*®, *Sight Reading and Rhythm Every Day*®, *Write, Play, and Hear Your Theory Every Day*®, and *The FJH Contemporary Keyboard Editions*, among others included in *The FJH Pianist's Curriculum*® by Helen Marlais, are designed to guide students from the beginner through advanced levels. Dr. Marlais has given pedagogical workshops in virtually every state in the country and presents showcases for FJH at the national piano teachers' conventions.

As well as being the Director of Keyboard Publications for The FJH Music Company, Dr. Marlais is also an Associate Professor of Music at Grand Valley State University in Grand Rapids, Michigan, where she teaches piano majors, directs the piano pedagogy program, and coordinates the young beginner piano program. She also maintains an active piano studio of beginner through high school age award-winning students.

Dr. Marlais has given collaborative recitals throughout the United States and in Canada, Italy, England, France, Hungary, Turkey, Germany, Lithuania, Estonia, China and Australia, and has premiered many new works by contemporary composers from the United States, Canada, and Europe. She has performed with members of the Chicago, Pittsburgh, Minnesota, Grand Rapids, Des Moines, Cedar Rapids, and Beijing National Symphony Orchestras and has recorded on Gasparo, Centaur and Audite record labels with her husband, concert clarinetist Arthur Campbell. She has also recorded numerous educational piano CD's on Stargrass Records®.

Dr. Marlais received her DM in piano performance and pedagogy from Northwestern University and her MFA in piano performance from Carnegie Mellon University.
Visit: www.helenmarlais.com

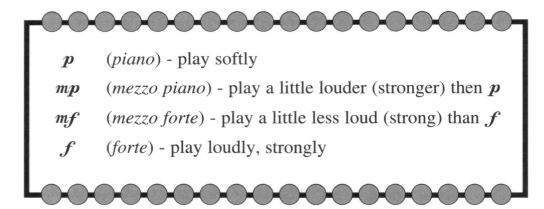

    p   (*piano*) - play softly

    mp   (*mezzo piano*) - play a little louder (stronger) then ***p***

    mf   (*mezzo forte*) - play a little less loud (strong) than ***f***

    f   (*forte*) - play loudly, strongly

FJH2200

TABLE OF CONTENTS

Unit 1

In this book, you will practice five techniques. Once they become a habit, you will play with beauty, speed, and ease!

1) Good Posture:

Playing with good posture is the Number 1 way to sound and feel good at the piano.

Sitting at the piano, imagine a daisy is growing
through your spine and out the very top of your head!
The daisy is gently pulling your body up until it is tall and balanced.

2) Arm Weight:

Don't wait for arm weight! Learning to drop your arm and wrist to the bottom of the key makes a beautiful, strong sound.

With your arms relaxed by your sides, close your
eyes and imagine that your arms are sandbags
and that sand is slowly drizzling from little holes
at the bottom of the sandbags onto the floor.

3) Flexible Wrists:

Playing with flexible wrists will help you play with easy and tension-free motions.

4) Free Arm:

Learning to shift your weight from one finger to the next will help you to play evenly as well as quickly. Remember that your arm moves freely when you play.

5) Strong Fingers:

Playing with strong fingers that do not dent at the first knuckle joint, is a must for all pianists!

4

Feeling Good Posture: The Snail Warm-Up

- Sit on the piano bench and slump, as if you are a snail rolled up in your shell.
- Slowly raise your back up until you are sitting tall and long. You are out of your shell.
- Sit tall when you play the piano.

Stepping Up and Stepping Down
(Playing 2nds)

Stepping Down and Stepping Up

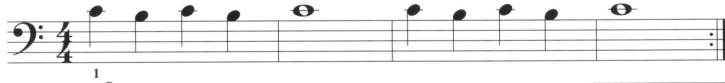

DID IT!

Walking in Big Boots

* Feel your arm weight and strong fingers as you play.

DID IT!

Walking in High Heels

* Play without dents in your fingers.

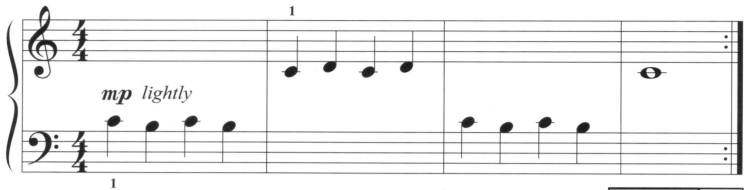

mp lightly

DID IT!

Three Steps Up and Then Back Down

mp

Three Steps Down and Then Back Up

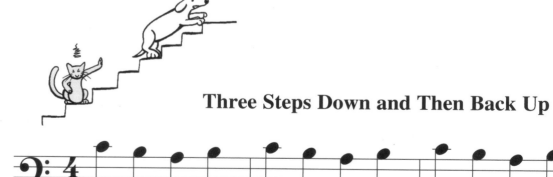

mp

DID IT!

FJH2200

Four Steps Up and Then Back Down

mp

Four Steps Down and Then Back Up

mp

You Go Up and I'll Go Down

mf

DID IT!

★ LESSON DAY

• Play your favorite piece of the week for your teacher. Then, your teacher may have you play another one.

Teacher comments: _____

Unit 2

Excellent Posture
Makes Everything Right

- Stand up and reach for the sky!
- Then drop your arms to your sides.
- Do it again. Doesn't that feel good?

Skipping Stones
(Playing 3rds)

DID IT!

Hop and Stop

* Play without dents in your fingers.

* Can you make the ♩ short and separated?

DID IT!

Rolling a Log

* Roll your right wrist in the direction of the notes.

Rolling a Log the Other Way

* Now roll your left wrist.

DID IT! ☐

Rolling Two Logs

Your thumbs play the same note!

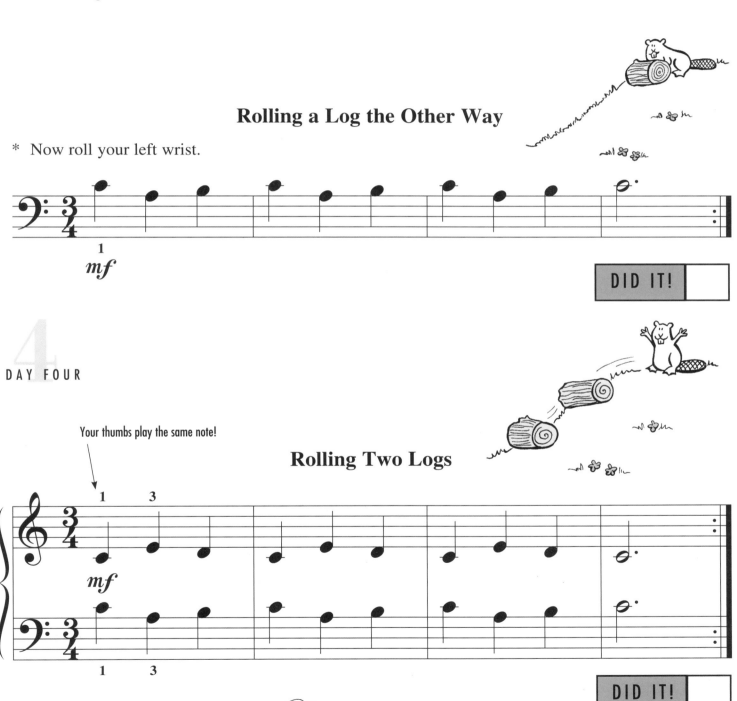

DID IT! ☐

* Have you been playing on the outside tip of your thumbnail? If so, great!

Up the Old Stone Stairs
(Repeated Notes)

Down the Old Stone Stairs
(Repeated Notes)

A Bird Saying No!

* Drop your arm into the keys without bouncing your wrists.
Notice your forearm, wrist, and hand moving together.

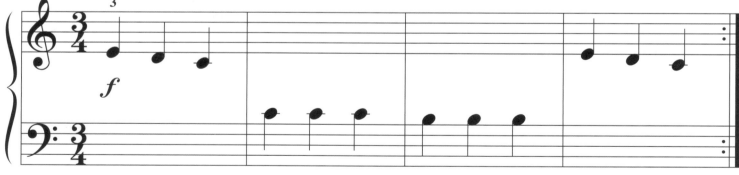

DID IT!

★ **LESSON DAY**

• Play your favorite piece of the week for your teacher. Then, your teacher may have you play another one.

Teacher comments: _____

FJH2200

Unit 3

Healthy Posture: Sandbag Arms

- Stretch your arms to the sides and reach, tensing up your arms! Then drop your arms to the sides and close your eyes, imagining that your arms are sandbags.
- Wait and notice how relaxed you feel.
- This relaxed feeling of arm weight is important when you play.

1 DAY ONE

2 DAY TWO

Walking Through Sand Dunes

* Drop your arm into the keys without bouncing your wrist. Notice your forearm, wrist, and hand moving together.

A Jumping Grasshopper

DID IT!

DID IT!

Inching Along

* Play with strong fingers that do not dent at the first knuckle joint.

DID IT!

The Ogre

* Drop your arm into the keys without bouncing your wrist. Notice your forearm, wrist, and hand moving together.

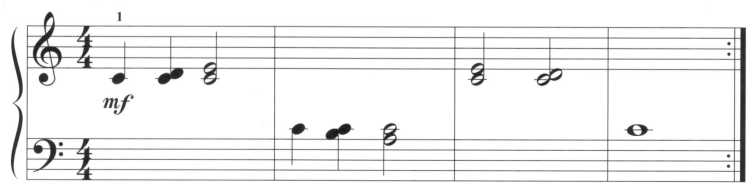

DID IT!

FJH2200

The Train Horn Blows!
(Playing 3rds)

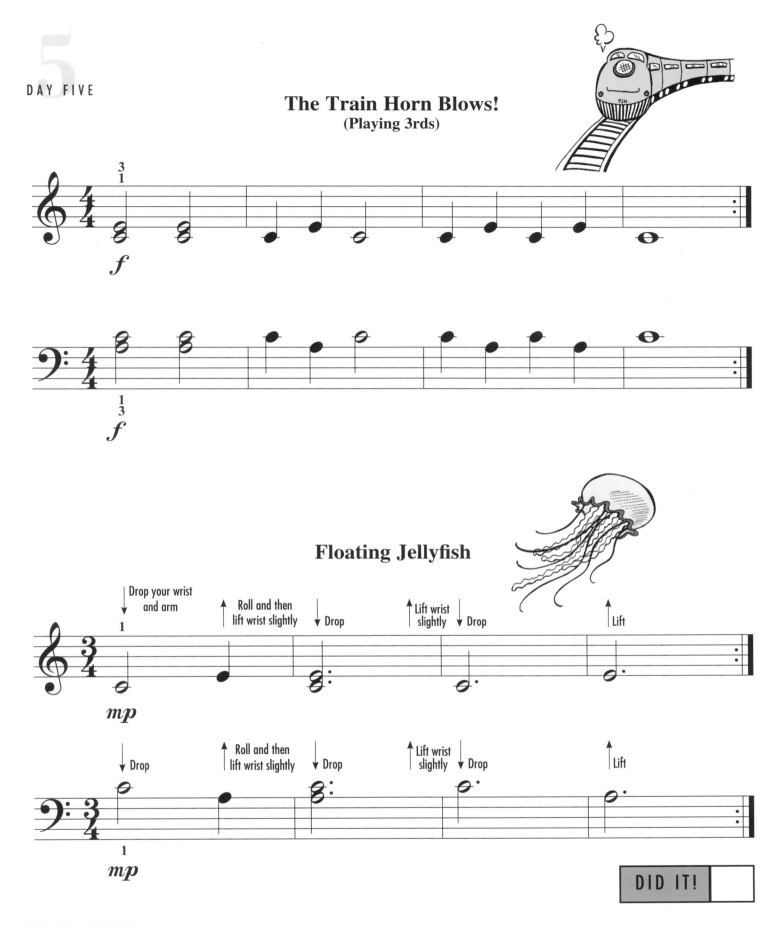

LESSON DAY

• Play your favorite piece of the week for your teacher. Then, your teacher may have you play another one.

Teacher comments: _____

Unit 4

Even Turtles Have Good Posture

- Raise your shoulders to your ears.
- Then relax your shoulders until they are low and wide.

Standing Up After Sitting

DID IT! ☐

The Mighty Lion

- Drop your arm into the keys without bouncing your wrist. Notice your forearm, wrist and hand moving together.

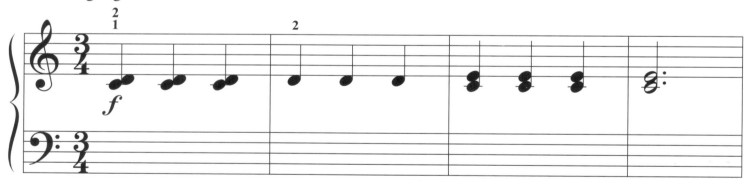

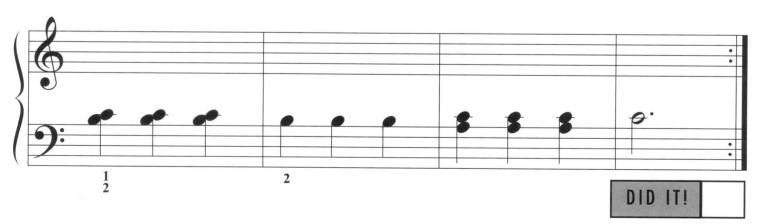

DID IT! ☐

3

The Cowboy

*R.H. over
the L.H.!*

* Play without dents in your fingers.

The Cowgirl

*L.H. over
the R.H.!*

DID IT!

4

Crisp Apples

* Make each ♩ sound crisp.

DID IT!

Listen!

Jumping on the Bed

* Drop your arm weight into the keys without bouncing your wrists. Notice your forearm, wrist, and hand moving together.

DID IT!

⭐ LESSON DAY

• Play your favorite piece of the week for your teacher. Then, your teacher may have you play another one.

Teacher comments: _____

DAY ONE

Healthy Posture:
Perfect Balance

- Sit on the piano bench.
- Place your feet on the floor or on a stool.
- Find your balance between your hip bones and your feet.

High Five!
(Guide Notes Middle C and Treble G)

mp

Down Low
(Guide Notes Middle C and Bass F)

mf

DID IT!

DAY TWO

Storm at Sea

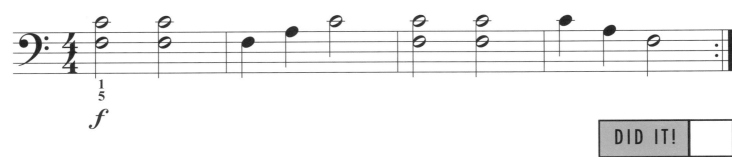

f

DID IT!

Shadows on the Wall

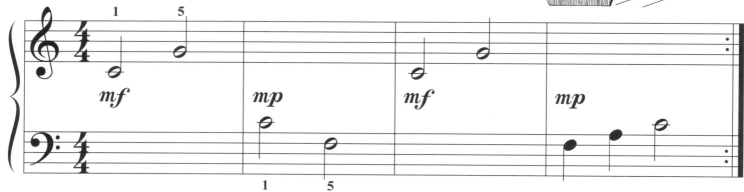

DID IT!

Light as a Feather

* Play each ♩ with a short, separated sound.

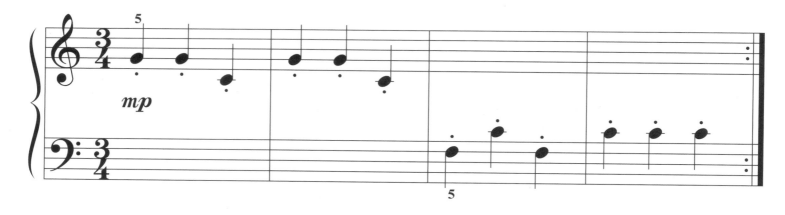

DID IT!

* ♩ ♪ = *staccato*

Mom's Dainty Dish

* Play the ♩ lightly on your fingertips.

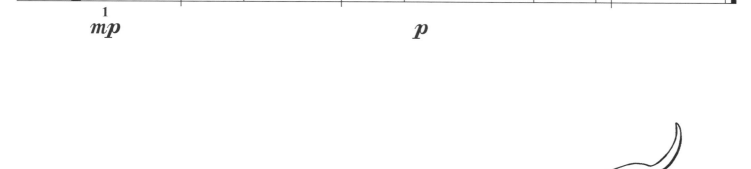

Jumping Over Hurdles

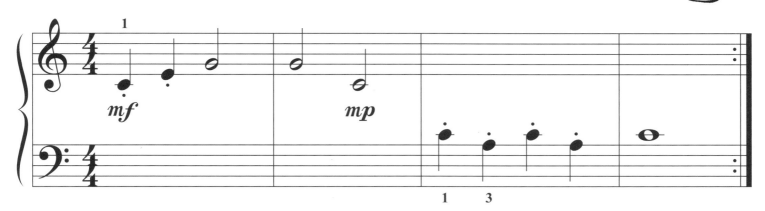

DID IT!

LESSON DAY

• Play your favorite piece of the week for your teacher. Then, your teacher may have you play another one.

Teacher comments: _____

Unit 6

Feeling Good Posture:
Playing with Power!

- Sitting on the piano bench, raise your arms to the keys.
- Notice where your elbows are.
- They should be **above** the tops of the white keys.
- You will be able to play with power when you sit at this height.

The Moose

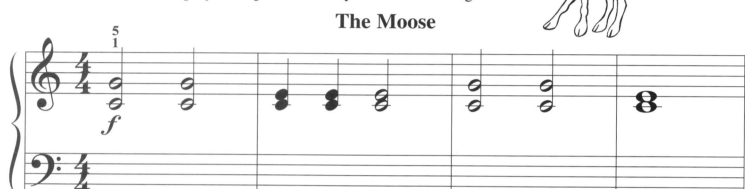

DID IT!

Two Moose Walking Together

DID IT!

FJH2200

A Grizzly Bear

DID IT!

Bubbles in the Tub

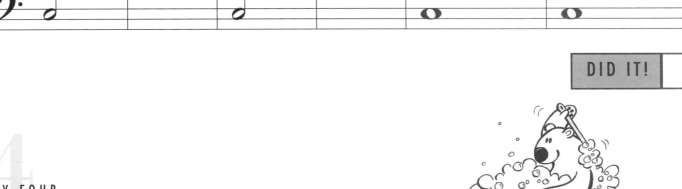

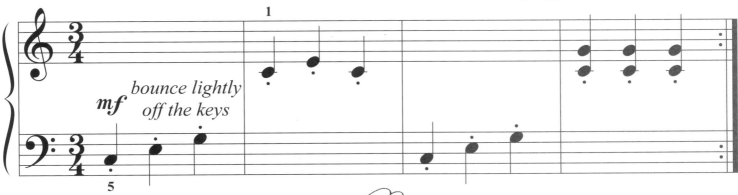

bounce lightly
off the keys

DID IT!

* Have you been playing on the outside tip
of your thumbnail? If so, super!

Scoops of Ice Cream

Making Sandcastles at the Beach

DID IT!

⭐ **LESSON DAY**

- Play your favorite piece of the week for your teacher. Then, your teacher may have you play another one.

Teacher comments: _____

Feeling Good Posture:
The Giraffe Warm-Up

- Imagine that your neck and spine are long and tall, like a giraffe.
- Walk around the room.
- Do you notice how good you feel?
- You are ready to make music today!

Down the Slide

* Roll your wrists to the left.

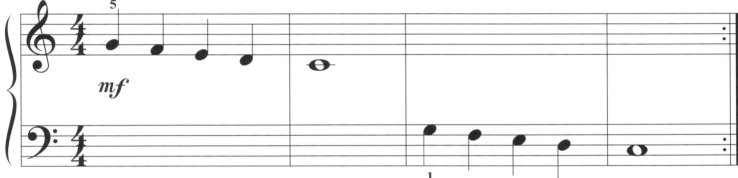

DID IT!

Swinging on the Swing

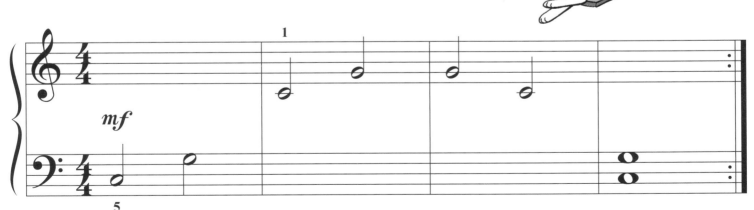

DID IT!

Dancing for Joy

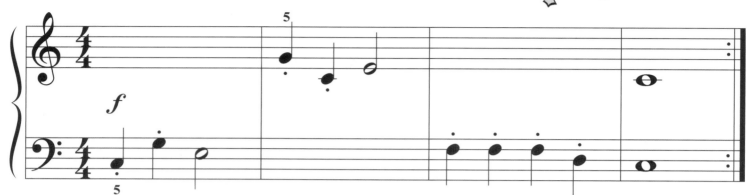

Throwing a Frisbee to the Right, and Then Throwing It to the Left

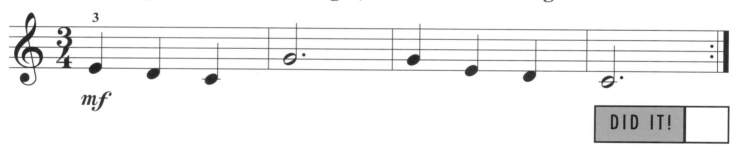

DID IT!

4
DAY FOUR

Mud Puddle Fun

* Drop your arm into the keys without bouncing your wrist. Notice your forearm, wrist, and hand moving together.

DID IT!

FJH2200

Monkey See, Monkey Do!

* Play without dents in your fingers.

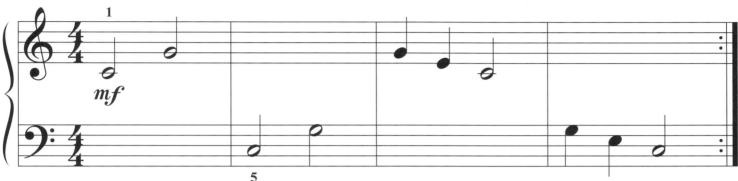

Snowflakes on My Face

* Play the ♩ lightly on your fingertips.

DID IT!

• Play your favorite piece of the week for your teacher. Then, your teacher may have you play another one.

Teacher comments: _____

Unit 8

Excellent Posture:
An Ocean Sponge

- Sit comfortably at the piano bench in the middle of the piano.
- Shift your weight to the right, then to the left.
- Do you notice that you are balanced on your hips as you move from side to side?
- Now come back to the center.
- You are ready to make music today!

The Sleepy Koala Bear

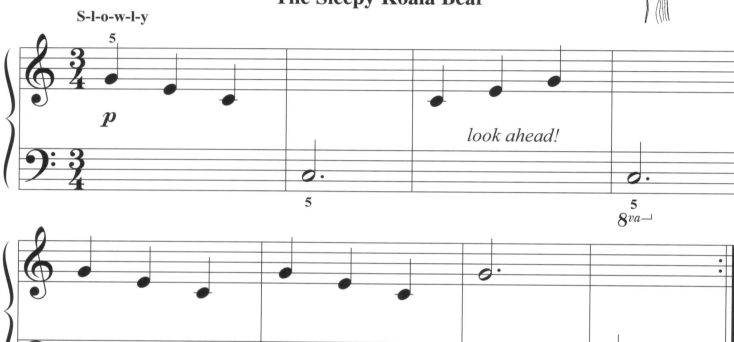

look ahead!

DID IT!

Laugh Like a Kookaburra

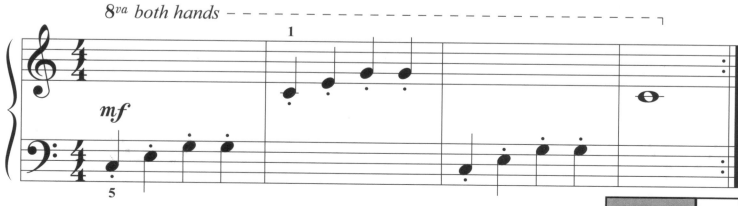

DID IT!

Drumming for Joy

Swinging by a Tail

* Roll your wrists in the direction of the notes.

8va both hands -

DID IT!

4

DAY FOUR

On Tip-Toe Through the House

8va 2nd time only -

DID IT!

Making Cartwheels

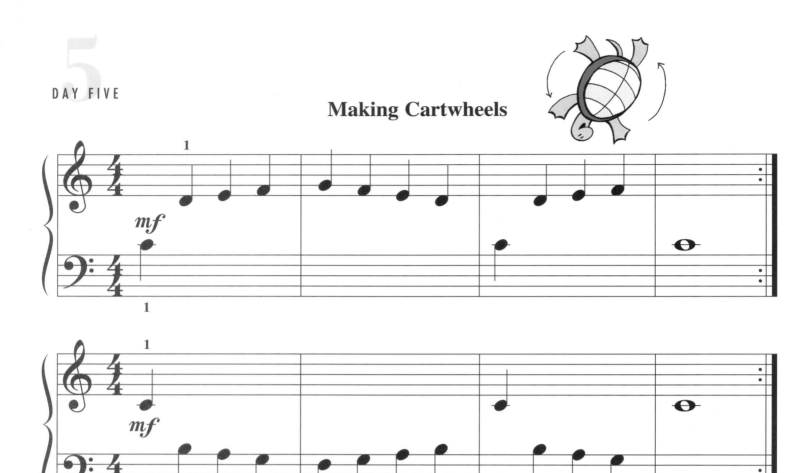

In an Echo Chamber

8va both hands   *8va both hands*

f   *move!*   *p*   *move!*   *f*   *move!*   *p*

DID IT!

• Play your favorite piece of the week for your teacher. Then, your teacher may have you play another one.

Teacher comments: _____

DAY ONE

Warming Up:
Making Snow Angels

- Sit tall and long on the piano bench.
- Make the "wings" of a snow angel in the air, up and then back down.
- Do you notice how good you feel?

Sticky Peanut Butter

* Drop your arm into the keys without bouncing your wrist.
   Notice your forearm, wrist, and hand moving together.

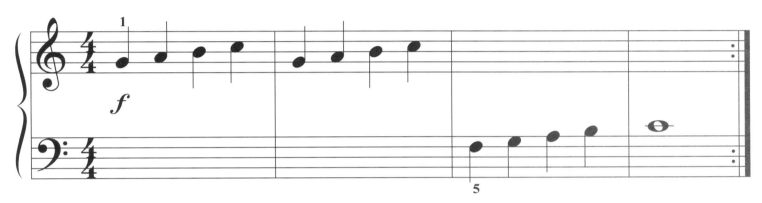

DID IT!

DAY TWO

Playing Ping-Pong

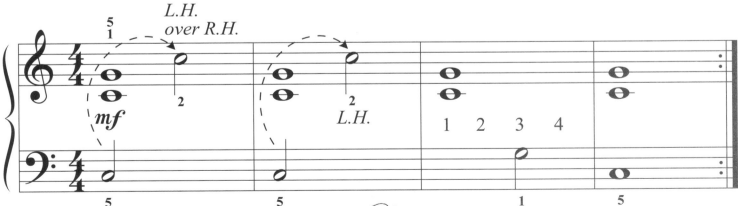

* Have you been playing on the outside tip
   of your thumbnail? If so, terrific!

DID IT!

Jack Rabbit

L.H.
over R.H.

This note is: ____

Riding My Bike Fast

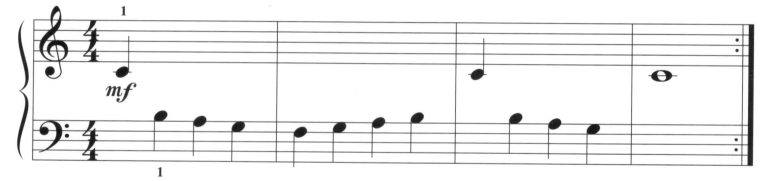

DID IT!

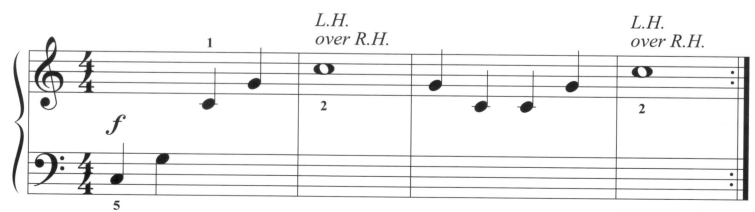

Soaring on a Magic Carpet

L.H.
over R.H.

L.H.
over R.H.

DID IT!

FJH2200

DAY FIVE

Sprinkles of Rain

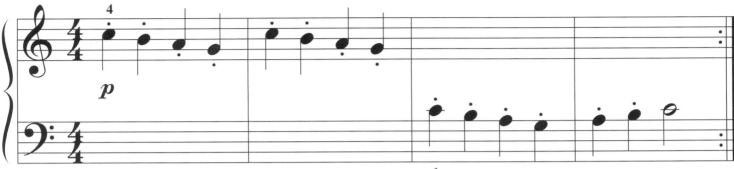

Watering Plants

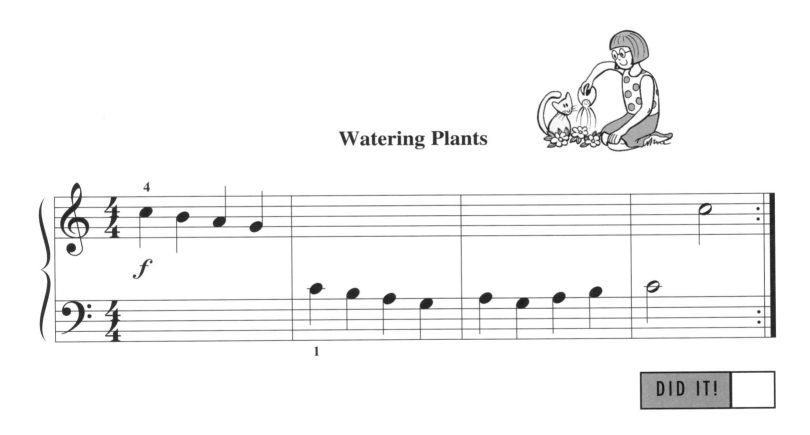

DID IT!

- Play your favorite piece of the week for your teacher. Then, your teacher may have you play another one.

Teacher comments: _____

Certificate of Achievement

_____

has successfully completed

ENERGIZE YOUR FINGERS EVERY DAY®
PREPARATORY

of The FJH Pianist's Curriculum®

You are now ready for **Book 1**

_____
Date

_____
Teacher's Signature